Bramlett

ONCE UPON A TIME

by

Eve Bunting

photographs by

John Pezaris

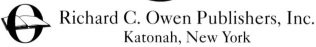

Richard C. Owen Publishers, Inc.
Katonah, New York

Meet the Author titles

Verna Aardema *A Bookworm Who Hatched*
David A. Adler *My Writing Day*
Frank Asch *One Man Show*
Joseph Bruchac *Seeing the Circle*
Eve Bunting *Once Upon a Time*
Lynn Cherry *Making a Difference in the World*
Lois Ehlert *Under My Nose*
Jean Fritz *Surprising Myself*
Paul Goble *Hau Kola Hello Friend*
Ruth Heller *Fine Lines*
Lee Bennett Hopkins *The Writing Bug*
James Howe *Playing with Words*
Johanna Hurwitz *A Dream Come True*

Karla Kuskin *Thoughts, Pictures, and Words*
Thomas Locker *The Man Who Paints Nature*
Jonathan London *Tell Me a Story*
George Ella Lyon *A Wordful Child*
Margaret Mahy *My Mysterious World*
Rafe Martin *A Storyteller's Story*
Patricia Mc Kissack *Can You Imagine*
Patricia Polacco *Firetalking*
Laurence Pringle *Nature! Wild and Wonderful*
Cynthia Rylant *Best Wishes*
Seymour Simon *From Paper Airplanes to Outer Space*
Jean Van Leewuen *Growing Ideas*
Jane Yolen *A Letter from Phoenix Farm*

Text copyright © 1995 by Eve Bunting
Photographs copyright © 1995 by John Pezaris

Richard C. Owen Publishers, Inc.
PO Box 585
Katonah, New York 10536

Library of Congress Cataloging-in-Publication Data

Bunting, Eve, 1928—
        Once upon a time / by Eve Bunting: photographs by John Pezaris .
        p . cm . - (Meet the author)
        ISBN 1-878450-59-X :
        1 .Bunting, Eve, 1928 - - Biography - Juvenile literature .
2 . Authors , American - 20th Century - Biography - Juvenile literature .
3 . Children's stories - Authorship - Juvenile literature .
[1 . Bunting, Eve, 1928—   2 . Authors , American . 3. Authorship .]
I . Pezaris, John,. , ill . II . Title . III . Series : Meet the author
(Katonah , N . Y .)
PS3552. U4735Z47 1995
813 ' . 54—dc20
                                                      94-47220
                                                        CIP
                                                        AC

Editor, Art, and Production Director   Janice Boland
Editorial/Production Assistant   Peter Ackerman
Color separations by Leo P. Callahan Inc., Binghamton, NY

Printed in the United States of America

9 8 7 6 5 4

To my granddaughters
Dana, Anna, Tory, and Erin

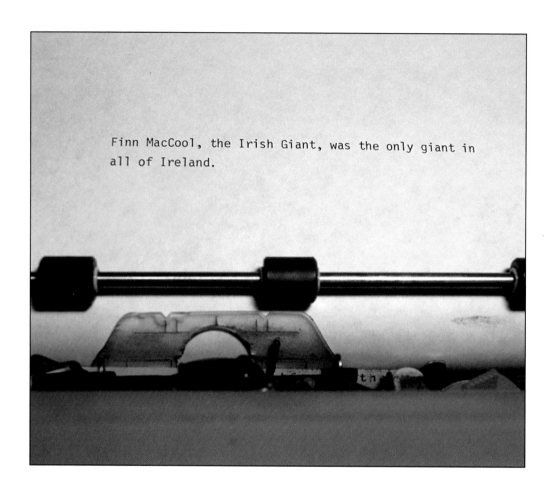

"Finn MacCool, the Irish giant, was the only giant in all of Ireland."

That was the first sentence in my first book.

I think I wrote that story because I love giants...
and I love Ireland.
That's where I was born, in this house
in a little town called Maghera.
My father had been born in this same house,
and my Grandfather Bolton before that.

Way back it had been a granary where farmers stored grain.
Sometimes, when we sat in the kitchen
there'd be a creak as the old house settled.
A small shower of seeds would drop down on us.
I always thought there was a ghost up there
playing tricks on us, and I'd say, "You up there! Stop that!"

I went to boarding school in Belfast, Ireland
when I was seven years old.
There were twelve girls in the dormitory where I slept.
After "lights out" we loved to tell stories,
especially scary ones.
I'd tell of my "ghost upstairs."
By then I'd convinced myself he was real.
I told how I could see his ghost eye
through the crack in the floorboards
each time I looked up!

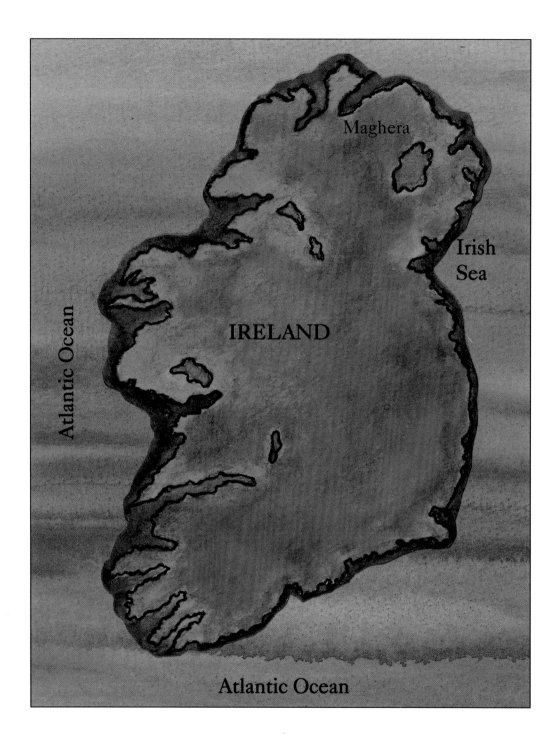

Maghera

Irish
Sea

Atlantic Ocean

IRELAND

Atlantic Ocean

When I went home from school for the holidays
I read a lot. That was partly because
it rains so much in Ireland.
The rain is what makes it so pretty and green.
My parents read to me, too.
Mostly my father read poetry out loud.
Poetry was his favorite.

"It was the schooner Hesperus,

That sailed the wintry sea;

And the skipper had taken his little daughter,

To bear him company,"

he'd read.
I'd know something terrible was coming in the poem
and I'd hide my face against his shoulder.

On sunny days we often went to the beach.
Here I am with my father on Portstewart Strand.
See my funny little cap?
I was just getting over mumps and was keeping warm.
We are both rather dressed up.
I think he'd taken me for "a breath of fresh air."
I'm sure there were books in our Austin car.
I don't remember,
but I'm sure it rained some time that day.
And I'm sure we sat in the car
and read to each other 'til the clouds passed.

When I grew up
and got married
I was lucky.
My new husband Ed
loved books too.
In 1959, Ed and I
and our three children left Ireland
and came to California.

The children were still little.
Christine was six, Sloan was two,
and Glenn was just a baby.
We were pretty brave. We didn't have work,
or money, or a house to come to.
But we knew this was the land of opportunity for us.
And it was.

I began to write when our children were all in school.
There was a little attic room in our first house
and I took it over.
We still live in that same, first house.
"Don't ever come up to this room
unless it's an emergency," I told my children,
"Mommy's writing." Mommy wasn't sure
if she could write, but she wanted to try.

I remember how they'd stand
at the bottom of the stairs and shout,
"It's an emergency! I can't find my shoes!"
or, "It's a true emergency!
Come see the drawing I did.
It's really good."

Still, I did write *The Two Giants*
and a hundred more books, besides.

My children grew up and moved away.
I brought my typewriter down from the attic
and settled into this room
with my desk and typewriter.

Always, though, I write my stories out first
in a notebook. That works best for me.
Pencils are easy to carry and I can take them any place I go.

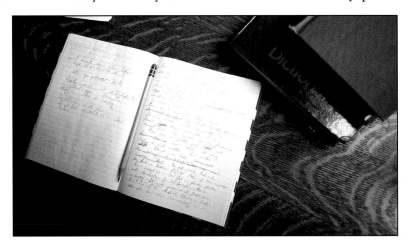

I have written in dentists' waiting rooms,
in my car during a traffic jam,
and in a floating chair in our swimming pool.

Sometimes I get an idea when
I don't have my notebook with me.
What a disaster!
But usually I can find something to write on.
Once I wrote a story on the back of a program
when we were at a play. It was dark.
Lucky for me I could still read the scrawl the next day!
Once, on an airplane, I started to write
a picture book on a "barf" bag.
I just hoped I wouldn't have to use the bag
for its *real* purpose!

Most of my ideas come from interesting things
that I've read in newspapers or magazines or books.
When I read about a beautiful oak tree in Texas
that was poisoned and died, I wrote *Someday a Tree*.

Another time I read a book
about the Vietnam Veterans
Memorial Wall
in Washington, D.C.
The pictures of visitors crying
as they left flowers and flags
beside the names
of those they'd loved
made me cry.
I wrote a picture book
called *The Wall.*
I cried as I wrote it.
And I'll tell you a secret.
I still cry when I read it.

Then I scold myself and say, "You wrote it, silly.
Why are you crying?" But I always cry.

Because I live in Los Angeles County
I was close to the awful city riots in 1992.
I wondered what it would be like
to be a child in those riots.
So I wrote a book called *Smoky Night*.
It is sad, too.
But at the end I try to show something important.
If people get to know each other
they may like each other.
And then they won't need to fight.

I hope some of the
sad books I write make
children think.
I hope some of the
"not sad" ones make
them laugh.
I hope I always write
books that children
will want to read.

One of my little granddaughters asked me,
"Are you writing another *once upon a time* book,
Grandma?"
She meant, "Are you writing a fairytale
or a folktale, like *The Two Giants*?"
What she asked made me smile.
But then I decided that most of my books
are *once upon a time* stories.

Once upon a time we destroyed trees.
I hope we will learn not to do that.

Once upon a time we went to war.
I hope we will learn that peace is better.

Once upon a time we didn't care about each other.
Let's try to care and understand.

Wouldn't that be a wonderful world for us to share?

Your friend,

Eve Bunting

Other Books by Eve Bunting

Night of the Gargoyles; *Flower Garden*; *A Day's Work*; *The Wednesday Surprise*; *How Many Days to America*; *In the Haunted House*.

About the Photographer

John Pezaris lives in Pasadena, California. He had lots of fun working on this book with Eve Bunting and her grandchildren. He planted the oak tree seedling shown on page 28 in a backyard in Pasadena. The photograph on page 24 was taken at the Vietnam War Memorial in Washington, D.C. John's advice to young photographers is, "always look for new ways to see things, never stop learning, and above all, don't be afraid to experiment."

Acknowledgments

Photographs on pages 5, 6, 9, 12, 14, and 15 appear courtesy of Eve Bunting. Photograph on top of page 19 appears courtesy of Eve Bunting. Illustration on bottom of page 18 by Eric von Schmidt, from *The Two Giants* by Eve Bunting, a MAGIC CIRCLE BOOK, copyright © 1985,1972, by Ginn and Company. Used by permission of Silver Burdett Ginn Inc. Illustration on page 24 from *The Wall* by Eve Bunting. Illustrations copyright © 1990 by Ronald Hilmer. Reprinted by permission of Clarion Books / Houghton Mifflin Co. All rights reserved. *The Wreck of the Hesperus* by Henry Wadsworth Longfellow. Map illustration by Janice Boland.